T0144954

WON BY ONE!

To order additional copies of this book, contact:
Xlibris
1-888-795-4274
www.Xlibris.com
Orders@Xlibris.com

Ceddy Keddy John and Tee Tee were in the house because there was a storm outside. Tee Tee said, "Since we can't play outside today, we should stay inside and read some books. I love reading but some words are spelled differently, but sound the same when you say them. I thought plurals and the S were tricky. But this is weird."

Ceddy Keddy John said, "Since we can't go outside today let's play a weird word game. I will tell you some words that sound the same but are spelled differently. You will have to spell the words back to me. I will give you clues about what the word means, too."

"I understand this weird word game. The last time we played basketball one-on-one, I won--W-O-N--by one--O-N-E."

Ceddy Keddy John said,"You got it right. Let's start the game. You know one plus one equals two. But there are three ways to spell 'to.' Here are the clues. Spell the number that is the answer to one plus one."

"That's easy... two--T-W-O."

"How do you spell the word when used for going from here to there?"

"To--T-O."

"What is the third one that means also?"

"I know this one. I read it once on dictionary.com. It means 'in addition.' That is too--T-O-O!"

"Tee Tee, after third period, what do you do? Also what is four plus four?"

"After third period I go eat, and four plus four equals eight—E-I-G-H-T."

"Tell me the past tense of 'eat'."

"The past tense of 'eat' is ate—A-T- E."

Ceddy Keddy John asked, "When you grow up what do you want to do?" And last summer what stung you? Also, it's the second letter of the alphabet, too."
"I want to be—B-E--the president when I grow up. I got stung by a bee—B-E-E--when we went hiking."

Ceddy Keddy John asked, "What kind of animal running very fast did we see when we went hiking?   Also, you wrote your brother a letter the next day. What was the first word in your brother's letter?"

"We saw a deer—D-E-E-R. I wrote my brother a letter, dear—D-E-A-R--Derrick."

"When you saw the deer, what did you want to do? Also, Mr. Jones' dog Frisky had a small bug on his neck called a--? "

"I wanted to run very fast. I wanted to flee--F-L-E-E--and Frisky had a flea--F- L- E- A--on his neck."

"Tee Tee, it looks like the rain stopped. We can go play outside now."

Tee Tee excitedly said, "Good...we can race to the field and I will pass you by--B-Y--and say good- bye—B-Y-E."

14

Ceddy Keddy John said, "You are fast, but can you beat me running?
I think the answer is no--N-O."
"I am faster than you think. After we race, you will know--
K-N-O-W--I can run faster than you."

Ceddy Keddy John said, "Tee Tee it is starting to rain again. We will have to race tomorrow."

"Tomorrow when--W-H-E-N--we race, I will win--W-I-N!"

END